Solos, Duets, and Trios with Piano A...

Favorite Wedding Classics

FOR FLUTE

CONTENTS

Editor: Carol Cuellar
Photography: Garry Gray

Copyright © 1992 CPP/Belwin, Inc.
15800 N.W. 48th Avenue, Miami, FL 33014

BRIDAL CHORUS
(From the opera "Lohengrin")

RICHARD WAGNER (1813-1883)
Arranged by KEITH SNELL

Con moto moderato

Flute 1

Flute 2

Flute 3

Bridal Chorus – 2 – 1

F3228FLX

Bridal Chorus – 2 – 2

WEDDING MARCH
(from the "Midsummer Night's Dream")

FELIX MENDELSSHON (1809-1847)
Arranged by KEITH SNELL

PRINCE OF DENMARK'S MARCH

JEREMIAH CLARKE (1674-1707)
Arranged by KEITH SNELL

Copyright © 1992 by BEAM ME UP MUSIC, c/o CPP/BELWIN, INC., Miami, FL 33014
International Copyright Secured   Made In U.S.A.   All Rights Reserved

Prince of Denmark's March – 3 – 3

F3228FLX

AIR
(From the "Water Music")

GEORGE F. HANDEL (1685-1759)
Arranged by KEITH SNELL

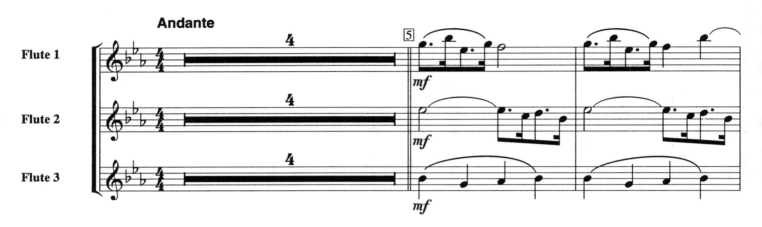

Air – 2 – 1
F3228FLX

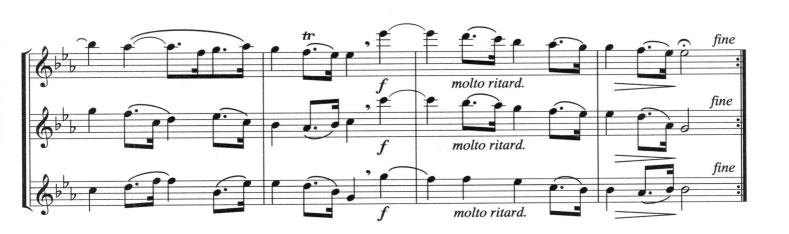

AVE MARIA
(Based on Prelude I from "The Well-Tempered Clavier")

JOHANN SEBASTIAN BACH (1685-1750)
Arranged by KEITH SNELL

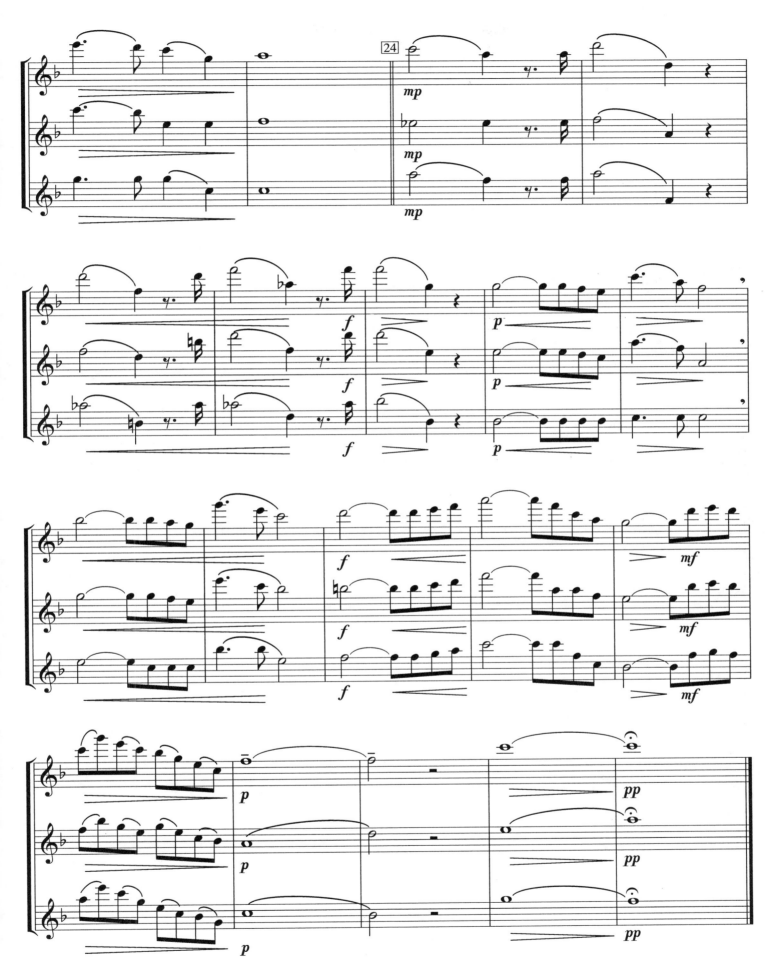

JESU, JOY OF MAN'S DESIRING
(Chorale Prelude from Cantata No. 147)

JOHANN SEBASTIAN BACH (1685-1750)
Arranged by KEITH SNELL

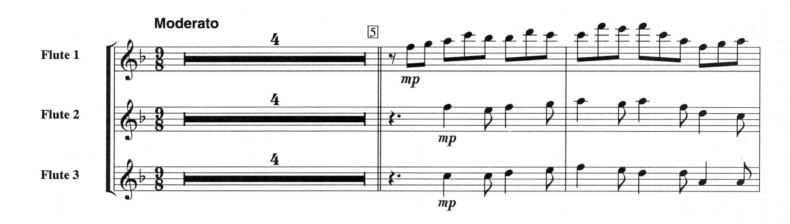

LET THE TRUMPETS SOUND!

(Chorus from Cantata No. 207)

JOHANN SEBASTIAN BACH (1685-1750)
Arranged by KEITH SNELL

Let The Trumpets Sound! – 3 – 2

F3228FLX

LA RÉJOUISSANCE
("The Rejoicing" from "Music For The Royal Fireworks")

GEORGE F. HANDEL (1685-1759)
Arranged by KEITH SNELL

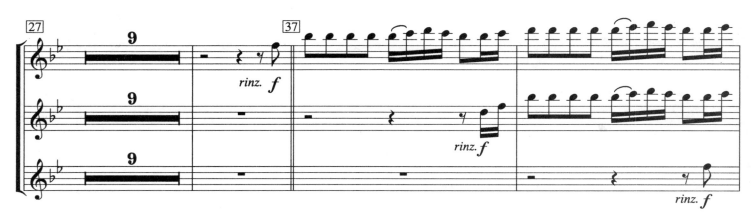

MARCH
(From "Judas Maccabaeus")

GEORGE F. HANDEL (1685-1759)
Arranged by KEITH SNELL

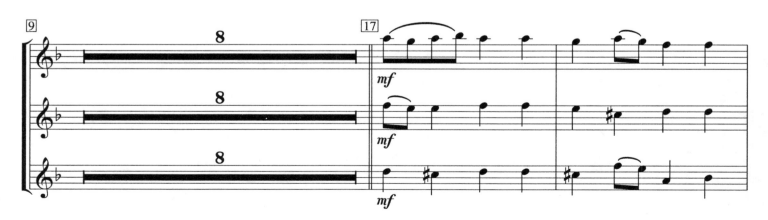

March – 2 – 1

F3228FLX

SARABANDE

JOHANN PEZEL
Arranged by KEITH SNELL

HORNPIPE
(from the "Water Music")

GEORGE F. HANDEL (1685-1759)
Arranged by KEITH SNELL

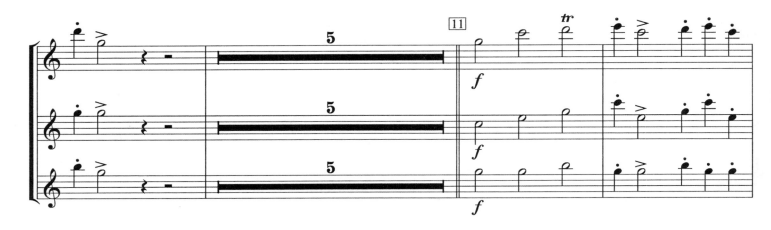

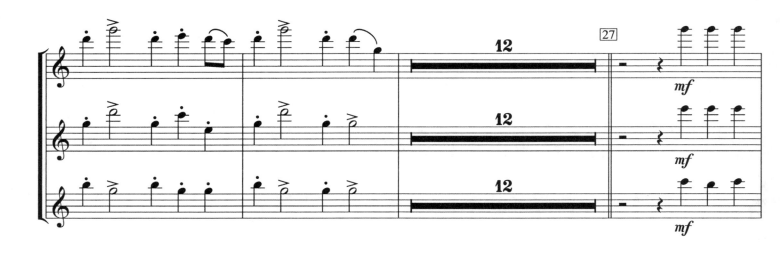

Hornpipe – 2 – 1
F3228FLX

BIST DU BEI MIR

("If Thou Be Near" from the Anna Magdelena Notebook)

JOHANN SEBASTIAN BACH (1685-1750)
Arranged by KEITH SNELL

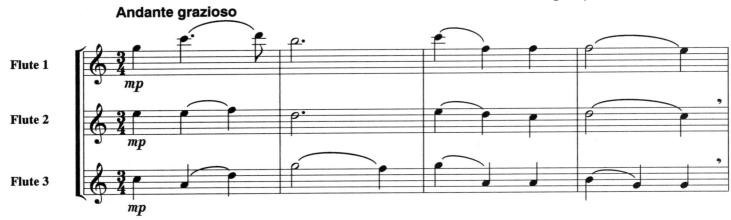

Bist Du Bei Mir – 2 – 1

F3228FLX

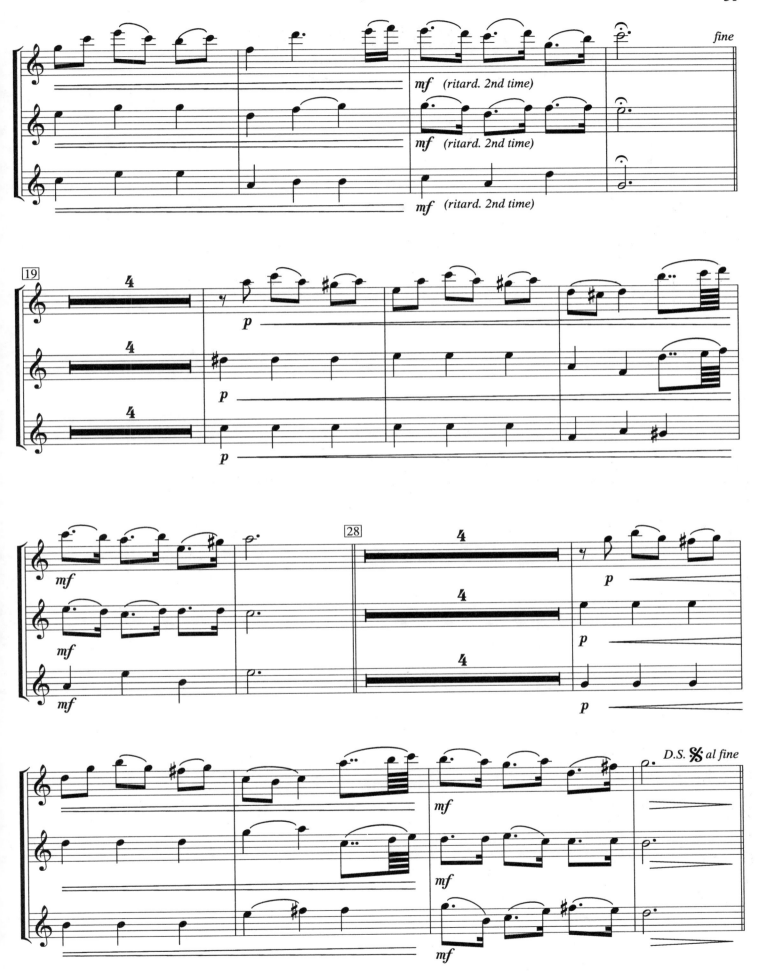

RONDEAU
(from "Symphonies Pour Le Roi")

JEAN JOSEPH MOURET (1682-1738)
Arranged by KEITH SNELL

Rondeau – 4 – 4
F3228FLX

TRUMPET TUNE

HENRY PURCELL (1659-1695)
Arranged by KEITH SNELL

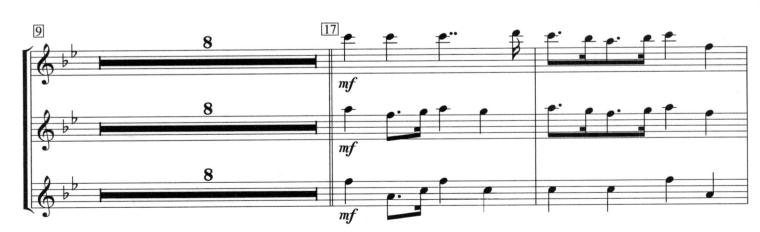

Trumpet Tune – 2 – 1
F3228FLX

PRELUDE
(From "Te Deum")

MARC-ANTOINE CHARPENTIER (1634-1704)
Arranged by KEITH SNELL

Prelude - 2 - 1

F3228FLX

15 POPULAR INSTRUMENTAL SOLOS

WITH CASSETTE

Just about anyone who plays a musical instrument wants to play popular music. This new series offers 15 great pop titles for fun and motivational playing. An accompaniment cassette tape comes with each book to help any instrument sound great! The piano/electronic keyboard edition also includes the melody line. All arrangements are written for **solo** or **unison** playing with any combination of these instruments.

_____ **Flute** (F2978FLT)
_____ **Clarinet** (F2978CLT)
_____ **Alto Saxophone** (F2978AST)
_____ **Tenor Saxophone** (F2978TST)
_____ **Trumpet** (F2978TRT)
_____ **Trombone** (F2978TBT)
_____ **Piano/Electronic Keyboard** (F2978PAT)

The 15 titles are:
- AFTER ALL (Love Theme from *Chances Are*)
- ALWAYS
- AMERICAN PIE
- DON'T WANNA LOSE YOU
- THE GREATEST LOVE OF ALL
- I HEARD IT THROUGH THE GRAPEVINE
- I JUST CALLED TO SAY I LOVE YOU
- LOVE THEME FROM *ST. ELMO'S FIRE*
- MISS YOU LIKE CRAZY
- THE PINK PANTHER
- THEME FROM *ICE CASTLES*
  (Through The Eyes Of Love)
- THEME FROM *TERMS OF ENDEARMENT*
- (I'VE HAD) THE TIME OF MY LIFE
- TONIGHT I CELEBRATE MY LOVE
- YOU'RE THE INSPIRATION

These books are also available without the cassette:

_____ **Flute** (F2978FLX)
_____ **Clarinet** (F2978CLX)
_____ **Alto Saxophone** (F2978ASX)
_____ **Tenor Saxophone** (F2978TSX)
_____ **Trumpet** (F2978TRX)
_____ **Trombone** (F2978TBX)
_____ **Piano Accompaniment** (F2978PAX)

This music is available from your favorite music dealer.